PRAISE FOR DAVID POSEN AND *THE LITTLE BOOK OF STRESS RELIEF*:

"It's amazing … not just a stress guide — it's a … Superb!"
— Rita Em… … rastinating Child

"No matter h… … nend to you Dr. Posen's *The L… heal … for stress management and is filled with great tips and insights. And it's fun to read! I plan to keep it handy, so I can re-read sections as the need arises."
— Peter G. Hanson, MD, author of *The Joy of Stress*

PRAISE FOR DAVID POSEN AND *STAYING AFLOAT WHEN THE WATER GETS ROUGH*:

"David Posen has done it again! His survival guide for changing times is down to earth, reassuring, and fun to read."
— Jack Canfield, co-author of *Chicken Soup for the Soul*

"David Posen is a very good advisor to anyone in transition. I recommend *Staying Afloat When the Water Gets Rough* to anyone who's trying to make it through a bad stretch of white water."
— William Bridges, author of *Transitions* and *Jobshift*

PRAISE FOR DAVID POSEN AND *ALWAYS CHANGE A LOSING GAME*:

"This book makes change seem fun rather than a chore. Dr. Posen shows you how to turn dreams into reality. Begin reading any page, you'll not want to put this wonderful book down."
— Christine A. Padesky, Ph.D., Director of The Center for Cognitive Therapy and co-author of *Mind Over Mood*

"For a change: a practical book full of the clinical wisdom of an experienced physician."
— Dr. Stanley E. Greben, Professor Emeritus of Psychiatry, University of Toronto

"This book is perceptive, instructive, productive, and written in an entertaining fashion. It is a valuable addition to any growing person's library."
— Dr. Ron Taylor, Toronto Blue Jays team physician and former major league baseball player

Also by David Posen, MD

Always Change a Losing Game
Staying Afloat When the Water Gets Rough
The Little Book of Stress Relief